Essex County Council

You can ask us to obtain books,
videos, C.D.s and cassettes which
are not in our stock —

enquire at your local library
for details

LAUNCH PAD
LIBRARY

ANCIENT
PEOPLES

CLAIRE FORBES

In association with
FRANKLIN WATTS

How to use this book

Cross references
Above the heading on the page, you will find a list of subjects in the book which are connected to the topic. Look at these pages to find out more about the subjects.

See for yourself
See for yourself bubbles give you the chance to test out some of the ideas in this book. They explain what you will need and what you have to do to see if an idea really works.

Quiz corner
In the quiz corner, you will find a list of questions. The answers to the quiz questions are somewhere on the two pages. Can you answer all the questions about each topic?

Glossary
Difficult words are explained in the glossary near the back of the book. These words are in **bold** on the page. Look them up in the glossary to find out what they mean.

Index
The index is at the back of the book. It is a list of words about everything mentioned in the book, with page numbers next to the words. The list is in the same order as the alphabet. If you want to find out about a subject, look up the word in the index, then turn to the page number given.

Contents

Discovering the past

Thousands of years ago, in ancient times, different groups of people lived in different places around the world. Each group had its own way of life. Many of these peoples are no longer here today, but they have left behind some of the things they used, such as buildings, coins and masks. We can learn a lot about ancient peoples by looking at these things.

Lost treasures

People who study objects to find out how ancient peoples lived are history detectives, called archaeologists. They cannot always build a complete picture of the people they are studying. This is because objects made from materials, such as wood or cloth, have rotted away.

▶ This ancient mask has lasted because it is made of a metal that does not rot away.

▲ This metal coin was used about two thousand years ago, by an ancient people called the Romans.

▶ These maps show the places where the ancient peoples in this book lived.

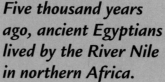

Five thousand years ago, ancient Egyptians lived by the River Nile in northern Africa.

Over two thousand years ago, ancient Greeks lived by the Mediterranean Sea.

4

 These stone **columns** and statues are part of the remains of an amazing city which was built in Central America in ancient times.

Quiz Corner

- Name two things that ancient peoples used that we can still see today.
- What do archaeologists study?
- Where did the Maya live?

Two thousand years ago, the Romans lived in the country we now call Italy.

About three thousand years ago, the ancient Chinese lived in east Asia.

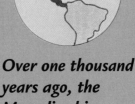

Over one thousand years ago, the Maya lived in Central America.

Over one thousand years ago, the Vikings lived in northern Europe.

5

look at: Egyptian beliefs, page 8

Ancient Egypt

About 5,000 years ago, the **civilization** of ancient Egypt stretched along the banks of the River Nile. The ancient Egyptians lived by the Nile because the river flooded every year, bringing water to fields where they grew food. The ancient Egyptian civilization lasted for about 3,000 years. During this time, people farmed the land, built towns and developed their own way of writing.

Town houses
Most ancient Egyptians lived in small, square houses built with mud bricks. Each house had small windows that let in a little light but kept out the heat of the sun. At night, the family slept on the flat roof, where it was cool.

▲ In ancient Egyptian writing, words and sentences were made up of pictures, which we call hieroglyphs.

▶ The busiest places in a town were markets. Here people did not pay with money but swapped goods with one another.

SEE FOR YOURSELF

Try writing using pictures. You can copy the examples below or make up your own. Try to make up enough picture words to write a secret message.

bird eye boat water

School and games

Most ancient Egyptian children did not go to school. Boys worked with their fathers and girls helped their mothers at home. In their free time, children played games such as leapfrog and tug-of-war.

▲ Ancient Egyptian children played with toys, such as this wooden horse. They also played with dolls and balls made of clay.

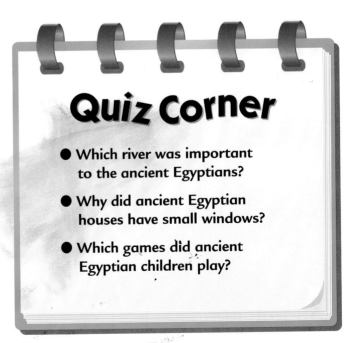

Quiz Corner

- Which river was important to the ancient Egyptians?

- Why did ancient Egyptian houses have small windows?

- Which games did ancient Egyptian children play?

look at: Ancient Egypt, page 6

Egyptian beliefs

Religion was very important to the ancient Egyptians. They prayed to many different **gods** to keep them safe from harm. The ancient Egyptians believed that they would go to a new world when they died. They were buried with things they might need for this new world, such as food and furniture.

Egyptian kings

The kings who ruled ancient Egypt were called pharaohs. A pharaoh was very powerful and treated like a god by the Egyptian people. When a pharaoh died, he was often buried inside an enormous tomb called a pyramid.

▼ Pyramids were built from heavy blocks of stone and took many years to finish.

Building a pyramid

Workers began building a pharaoh's pyramid long before he died. They dragged heavy blocks of stone up a ramp to the building site, using ropes and logs. Then each stone was put into place.

ramp

stone block

logs

CHATTERBOX

One of the most important **goddesses** to the ancient Egyptians was called Isis. Egyptian women believed that Isis would look after them in their daily life.

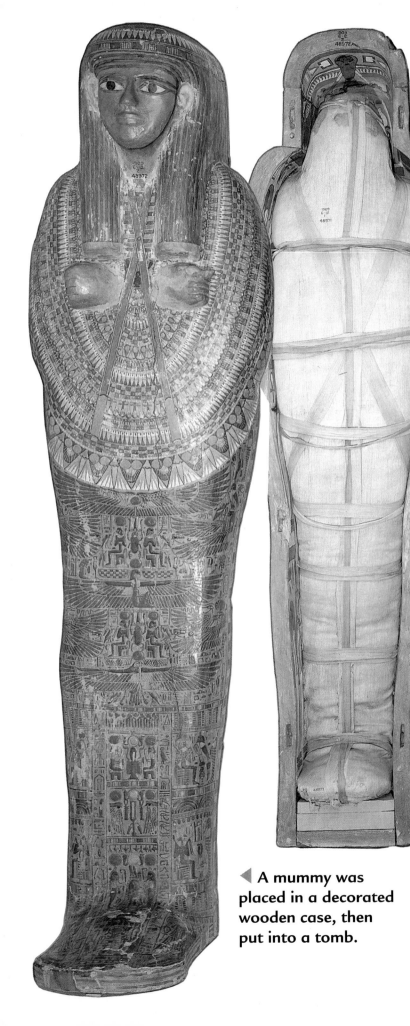

Making mummies

Ancient Egyptians believed they would need their bodies in the next life. When pharaohs and rich people died, their bodies were dried, preserved with salts, and wrapped in bandages to stop them from rotting. Bodies kept like this are called mummies.

Egyptian cats

Cats were holy animals to the ancient Egyptians. When a pet cat died, the owner shaved off his own eyebrows to show how sad he was.

▶ Mummies of cats have been found buried in the tombs of ancient Egyptians.

◀ A mummy was placed in a decorated wooden case, then put into a tomb.

Quiz Corner

● What were ancient Egyptian kings called?

● Which animals were holy to the ancient Egyptians?

● How were mummies made?

Ancient Greece

Over 2,000 years ago, the land of Greece was divided into **city states**. Each city state had its own city, farmland, army and laws, or rules. The city state of Athens was famous for learning and **drama**, while Sparta was famous for its army. The ancient Greeks were the first people to **vote** for their rulers.

Greek plays

The first plays were put on in Athens. They were performed during religious festivals in huge open-air theatres. All the parts of the play were acted by men, who wore masks to show different kinds of character.

SEE FOR YOURSELF

Make your own Greek mask using a white paper plate. Ask a grown-up to help you cut out the eyes, mouth and nose, and to make a small hole at each side. Paint your mask. Then thread elastic through the small holes and tie a knot at each side.

A group of actors, called the chorus, explained what was happening in the play.

At school

A Greek boy went to school from the age of seven until fifteen. His parents had to pay for his lessons, so a boy from a poorer family did not stay at school for long. A Greek girl did not go to school. She was taught how to cook and run a house by her mother.

In Athens, schoolboys were taught reading, writing, maths, sports, poetry and music. But in the city state of Sparta, school-life was different. Boys were taught to fight, steal and lie to make them cunning soldiers.

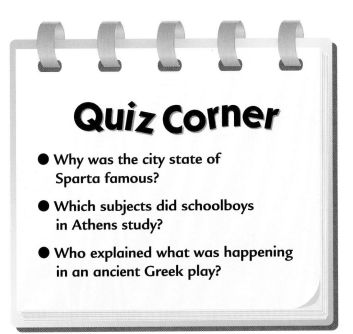

▲ Schoolboys did not have paper and pencils, but used a pointed stick, called a stylus, to scratch on to a layer of wax in a wooden frame.

People's jobs

Many ancient Greek men were farmers or craftsmen. Women and young girls looked after the house, prepared food and made clothes. Rich Greek men and women kept **slaves** to help them with their work. Greek women and slaves had no say in how their city state was run.

Sometimes Greek plays lasted all day, so the actors needed good memories.

◀ During a play, the audience sat on steps around the stage. Poor people paid less than rich people for the same seats.

Quiz Corner

- Why was the city state of Sparta famous?

- Which subjects did schoolboys in Athens study?

- Who explained what was happening in an ancient Greek play?

11

look at: Ancient Greece, page 10

Life in Greece

The ancient Greeks are famous for many things. They carved beautiful statues and built huge stone buildings and **temples**. They also invented a sporting contest, called the Olympic Games, which still takes place today. We have learnt many things from the ancient Greeks, including ideas about science, **government**, maths and medicine.

CHATTERBOX

The Greeks made up many stories about their gods and **goddesses**. One story tells how Athena, the goddess of war, was born. It says that one day the god Zeus was hit on the head, his head cracked open and out jumped Athena.

Olympic Games

Every four years, the Olympic Games took place at Olympia on the west coast of Greece. The games were held in honour of the Greek **god**, Zeus. People came from all over Greece to take part in sporting events, such as boxing, running, wrestling and javelin throwing.

▶ This picture from a vase shows a man riding a **chariot** pulled by horses. Chariot races were held at the ancient Olympic Games.

Winning the Olympics
On the last day of the Games, winners were given a crown woven from the leaves of olive trees. There was also a big feast and a huge celebration.

▲ In one Olympic event, men threw a discus, or bronze disc, as far as they could.

Greek columns

Buildings in ancient Greece often had tall, straight **columns**. Today, only a few ancient Greek buildings are left, but many towns around the world have buildings in a similar style.

▲ This Greek temple is called the Parthenon. It was built in Athens for the goddess, Athena.

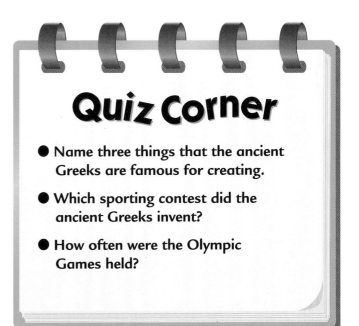

Quiz Corner

- Name three things that the ancient Greeks are famous for creating.

- Which sporting contest did the ancient Greeks invent?

- How often were the Olympic Games held?

look at: The Roman army, page 16

Ancient Rome

About 2,000 years ago, the Romans ruled many lands around the Mediterranean Sea, including the country we now call Italy. These lands made up the Roman **Empire**. The Romans built many towns and cities in their empire. The largest and most important city was Rome.

Town houses
In Rome, rich Romans lived in large town houses with gardens. They had **slaves** to look after them. Poor Romans lived in tiny flats, without running water or kitchens.

◀ Mosaics were made out of tiny pieces of coloured stone. Rich Romans decorated their floors with them.

SEE FOR YOURSELF
Here's an easy way to make a mosaic. Draw the outline of a picture on a piece of stiff paper. Cut sheets of different coloured paper into lots of small squares. Stick the squares on to the paper inside your outline.

Most Romans washed in a public bathhouse.

In a huge arena, people watched contests and other entertainment.

People could collect drinking water from a fountain in the street.

▲ Some Roman towns were full of grand buildings, such as **temples**, theatres and public baths.

*People gathered in the **forum**, or town square, to have meetings and buy or sell things.*

*Inside a Roman temple there were statues of **gods**. People gave gifts to the gods to bring themselves good luck.*

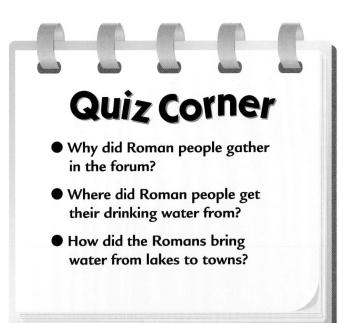

▲ The Romans built bridges to carry water from lakes to the towns. This bridge carried water to the city of Nîmes in France.

Carrying water

Bridges which carried water were called aqueducts. Water flowed along pipes built into the top of the aqueduct. In the town, water that had been used was carried away in pipes beneath the streets.

Quiz Corner

● Why did Roman people gather in the forum?

● Where did Roman people get their drinking water from?

● How did the Romans bring water from lakes to towns?

look at: Ancient Rome, page 14

The Roman army

The Roman army was the most successful army of ancient times. It protected the **Empire** and made sure that everyone living there followed Roman laws, or rules. The army was made up of trained soldiers from all over the Empire. The soldiers built roads, linking the towns and cities in the Empire.

Foot soldiers

Most Roman soldiers travelled on foot. Each one carried a short sword, a dagger, a spear and a shield. A soldier wore a helmet on his head and metal armour over his chest to protect himself. Strips of leather covered with metal hung from his belt. These clanked loudly when he walked and helped to frighten his enemies.

Under a shell

In battle, soldiers locked their shields together to make a kind of shell around themselves. This protected the soldiers from rocks and spears thrown by enemies.

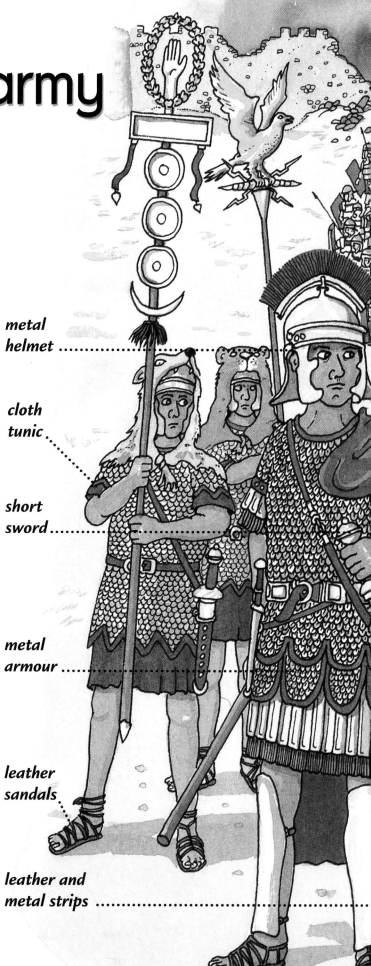

metal helmet ....

cloth tunic ....

short sword ....

metal armour ....

leather sandals ....

leather and metal strips ....

Over the walls

Soldiers used wooden towers to break into an enemy town. They climbed up the towers and fought their way over the town's walls. Soldiers also fired rocks from a giant catapult to knock down the walls.

.... *catapult*

shield

Soldier's backpack

When a foot soldier was marching, he carried everything he needed in a backpack. Inside, he had cooking pots, bedding and enough food to last for up to three days.

Quiz Corner

● How did groups of Roman soldiers use their shields to protect themselves?

● How did Roman soldiers break into an enemy town?

look at: Chinese inventions, page 20

Ancient China

Until a few hundred years ago, the way of life in China hardly changed at all. Most people were farmers who lived in the countryside. They worked hard growing food. Others worked as crafts-people or **merchants**. A ruler, called an emperor, **governed** the country, with the help of officials.

▲ Chinese farmers have grown and eaten rice for thousands of years.

Chinese food

Farmers were important because they grew food for the many thousands of people who lived in ancient China. Most people ate vegetables, millet and rice, but the emperor and other rich people often ate much more expensive food, such as sharks' fins and bears' paws.

▶ Jugglers and musicians entertained the emperor at feasts.

Family life

In most Chinese families, children, parents and grandparents all lived together in the same house. Parents and elders were very strict with children, and wives were expected to obey their husbands.

The ancient Chinese believed that over-hanging roofs would keep bad spirits out of the building. Many roof tiles were also painted to scare away evil spirits.

Tomb treasures

The ancient Chinese believed in life after death. When the emperor died, he was buried with models of horses, servants and **chariots**. He hoped that these models would help him in his new life.

▲ When China's first emperor died, he was buried with 7,000 life-size terracotta models of soldiers to protect him.

Quiz Corner

● Why did the ancient Chinese have over-hanging roofs?

● Who were the people of ancient China ruled by?

● Why were China's emperors buried with models of horses, servants and chariots?

look at: Ancient China, page 18

Chinese inventions

The ancient Chinese were brilliant inventors. They made their own paper and developed a way of printing using wooden blocks. Other countries did not develop these things until hundreds of years later. The Chinese also invented wheelbarrows, umbrellas and playing cards.

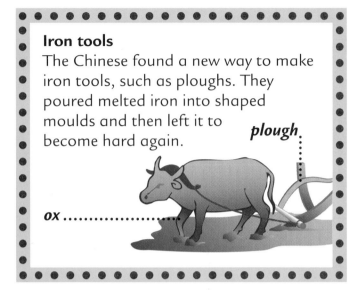

Iron tools
The Chinese found a new way to make iron tools, such as ploughs. They poured melted iron into shaped moulds and then left it to become hard again.

plough

ox

▲ The first fireworks were made by the Chinese. They used gunpowder to fire the fireworks into the air.

Land of silk
The Chinese made a fine cloth called silk. They **traded** silk with other people in Asia. Chinese silk was so popular that the Romans called China 'Serica', which means 'land of silk'.

▶ Rich people wore beautiful silk robes. This robe belonged to the wife of an emperor.

Enemy attacks
The Great Wall was built to protect China from attacks by invaders from the north. It took thousands of people hundreds of years to build it.

▼ The Great Wall of China is the longest wall in the world. In the past, guards walked along the path on the top of the wall and lit warning fires if enemies attacked.

Quiz Corner

- Name three things that the ancient Chinese invented.

- Why was ancient China called 'land of silk'?

- Why did the ancient Chinese build the Great Wall of China?

look at: Life in Maya times, page 24

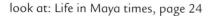

The Maya

Over 1,000 years ago, an ancient people called the Maya made their home in Central America. They lived in **city states**, which were made up of a city, nearby villages and farmland. The Maya were expert **astronomers**. They also developed their own way of counting and writing using pictures.

Maya cities

The Maya built great stone cities with huge pyramids, palaces and **temples**. They often covered their temples with shiny white plaster or painted them bright red. Sometimes Maya cities went to war with each other. When enemies were captured, they were made into **slaves**.

▲ Maya temples were built on top of high, flat-topped pyramids in the centre of the city. These temples are in the ancient city of Uxmal in Mexico.

Pleasing the gods

The Maya believed in many different **gods** and prayed to them every day for help with their daily tasks. They also held special **ceremonies** for their gods. Sometimes a ball game called pok-a-tok was played at these ceremonies.

▶ Pok-a-tok was played on a ball court inside the city. Players hit a rubber ball through a stone ring at one end of the court, using only their elbows or hips.

◀ Today, only a few Maya books are left. They are kept in museums.

Maya books

The Maya wrote on long strips of tree bark which they folded into pages and made into books. The covers of the books were made from jaguar skins. The Maya wrote with brushes or feathers dipped in different coloured inks.

Quiz Corner

- How did the Maya make books?
- Which kinds of buildings could you find in a Maya city?
- What did the Maya write on?
- What was pok-a-tok?

look at: The Maya, page 22

Life in Maya times

Most Maya people were farmers, who grew crops for food and kept bees for honey. They also hunted animals to eat. The Maya lived in simple huts. Girls stayed at home with their mothers and learned how to look after a family. Maya boys were sent away to special houses where they learned about fighting and war.

avocado

Maya food

The Maya grew corn, beans, chilli peppers and fruit, such as papayas and avocados. They also planted cacao trees, which gave them cocoa beans for making chocolate. Cocoa beans were sometimes used as money.

papaya

chilli pepper

Growing corn

Corn was the most important food for the Maya. They ate it as part of nearly every meal. For breakfast, the Maya ate a thin porridge which was made from ground corn. Workers in the fields ate corn dumplings.

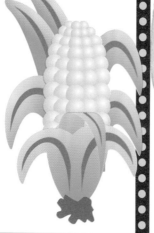

Working life

Maya women prepared food and made clothes at home. They also grew crops. Maya men went hunting, using bows and arrows to kill large animals, such as deer.

◀ Maya women wove cotton on tall wooden looms. They ground corn into flour using special grinding stones.

Maya calendars

The Maya had several **calendars** to help them count days and years. They believed that some days on the calendars were unlucky. On these days, the Maya tried to do as little work as possible.

▲ This statue has pictures of animals and **gods** carved into it to show important events in Maya times.

CHATTERBOX

The Maya believed that the Sun and the planet Venus played an important part in their lives. They thought that the position of Venus when a child was born, helped shape his or her character.

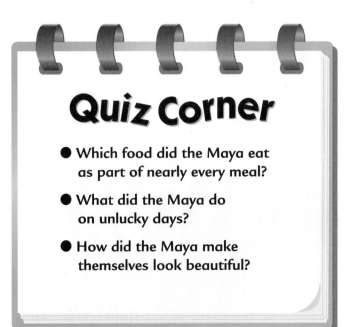

Maya make-up

To make themselves look beautiful, the Maya filed their front teeth into sharp points and filled the gaps with pieces of a hard green stone called jade. Married men and women also decorated their bodies with tattoos from the waist up. Unmarried men and warriors painted their bodies black. Unmarried women painted their bodies red.

Quiz Corner

- Which food did the Maya eat as part of nearly every meal?
- What did the Maya do on unlucky days?
- How did the Maya make themselves look beautiful?

The Vikings

Over 1,000 years ago, the Vikings lived in a part of northern Europe called **Scandinavia**. Their lands were crowded, so they built wooden ships and sailed to other countries. Some Vikings were warriors and attacked these countries, but many were traders, who set up new towns in the places where they settled.

◀ Rich Viking sailors wore iron helmets such as this one. Poorer Vikings had to make do with leather caps.

Warships

Large Viking ships were called longships. They were light and travelled quickly. Longships could sail up rivers, as well as across seas. Each longship had a sail, oars for rowing and a wider, heavier oar at the back for steering. Inside the ship, there were boxes where Viking sailors kept weapons, such as swords and axes.

▶ The front of a Viking ship was usually carved into the shape of a bird, serpent or dragon.

CHATTERBOX

When rich Vikings died, they were often put in a ship filled with their belongings. Then the ship was buried in the ground or burned.

Land travel

In summer, Vikings rode on horses or in carts pulled by horses or oxen. In winter when snow covered the ground, they travelled on sledges, skis or ice skates.

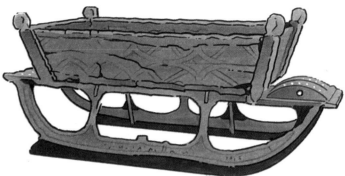

▲ Sledges were used to pull heavy loads, such as firewood, over the icy ground.

Crossing the ocean

The Vikings were brave explorers. They were the first people from Europe to sail across the Atlantic Ocean to North America. The Vikings made their homes in many of the places they travelled to, including Iceland, Greenland and Britain.

Quiz Corner

- Where did the Vikings come from?
- Which places did the Vikings explore?
- Name two Viking weapons.
- In winter, how did Vikings travel on land?

look at: The Vikings, page 26

Viking life

Vikings were farmers and fishermen as well as sailors. They grew food, hunted wild animals for their meat and skins and caught fish to eat. They also kept sheep and cattle. When the men were away at sea, women ran the farms and wove cloth for sails, blankets and clothes.

Writing and storytelling

The Viking alphabet had 16 letters called runes. Each rune was made up mostly of straight lines, which were easier to carve into wood or stone than curved lines. The Vikings used the runes to write messages. Long stories were usually learned by heart and told aloud rather than written down.

▲ Most Viking houses were made of wood, but some were made from stone or earth.

At home

A Viking family lived in a long house, which had only one room and no windows. A fire was kept burning in the middle of the room for heat, light and cooking food, such as stew. Most people slept and ate on benches around the edges of the room. Outside the house, there were workshops and sheds where animals were kept.

▲ This ancient Viking stone has runes carved in a border around its edges.

Sagas

Viking children were taught at home. They were told long stories, or sagas, about the adventures of the **gods** or of great Viking heroes. Storytellers travelled around telling sagas aloud at feasts and festivals. They were especially popular on cold, winter nights when everyone sat inside the house around the fire.

SEE FOR YOURSELF

Viking clothes had no buttons, zips or poppers. They were held together by brooches and belts. Look at your clothes and see how many different ways there are of doing them up.

Viking crafts

The Vikings were skilled crafts-people who carved and decorated all kinds of materials. They made combs, spoons and ice skates from animal bones, and tents and sleeping bags from animal skins. Jewellery, such as rings, was made from gold, silver and bronze. Necklaces had amber, glass or jet beads. The Vikings also made pots on pottery wheels.

Quiz Corner

● Who looked after the farm when the Viking men were away?

● How many rooms were there in a Viking house?

● What are the letters of the Viking alphabet called?

carved drinking horn

comb carved from bone

silver spoon

▶ Vikings enjoyed playing and listening to music. This girl is playing a carved wooden pipe.

Amazing facts

● Viking soldiers believed that they would go to a place called Valhalla if they died in battle. Valhalla was a type of paradise, where they could fight all day and hold feasts all night.

☆ *The Great Pyramid was built in Egypt in ancient times, but most of it is still standing today. It is made from over two million different blocks of stone.*

● At the funerals of some rich ancient Greeks, people were paid to cry for the dead. Their tears were collected and kept in a jar called an amphora.

☆ *The ancient Egyptians didn't have knives or forks, so they ate with their fingers. A pharaoh had a servant to wash his hands between each course of a meal.*

● Roman men did not usually grow beards. But when an emperor called Hadrian grew a beard, men in Roman lands copied him and grew beards too.

☆ *In ancient China, men and women grew their hair long and wore it in a bun on top of their heads. They cut it only when a member of their family died.*

● Romans flavoured their food with liquamen, which was made from the insides of fish. The fish were mixed with salty water and left to rot in the sun.

☆ *The Maya thought that flat heads and crossed eyes were beautiful. A baby's head was strapped between two boards to flatten it. Older children had a bead dangled in front of their eyes to make them cross-eyed.*

● The three Fates were important goddesses in ancient Greece. People believed that the Fates decided whether they would live or die.

☆ *There is an old Chinese legend, or story, which says that the Great Wall of China is not a wall at all, but a huge dragon which has turned to stone.*

Glossary

astronomer Someone who studies the stars, planets and Sun.

calendar A list which shows the days, weeks and months in a year.

ceremony A special act carried out by people to mark an occasion.

chariot A two-wheeled cart which is usually pulled by horses.

city state A city and the surrounding farms, villages and houses ruled by it.

civilization A group of people with its own set of laws, **government**, and customs.

column A tall, round post, used to support or decorate a building.

drama A play which is acted on a stage in front of an audience.

empire A group of lands or countries under one ruler.

forum The main square of an ancient Roman town, where important business took place.

god/goddess Someone to whom a person prays.

govern To rule a country.

government The group of people who are in charge of a country.

merchant A person who buys, sells or swaps goods to make money.

Scandinavia The name for an area of land including Norway, Sweden and Denmark.

slave A servant who belongs to another person and who has no rights.

temple A building where people go to worship a **god**.

trade To buy, sell or swap goods.

vote To choose something or someone, such as a law or a ruler.

Index

Created by:
Two-Can Publishing Ltd
346 Old Street
London EC1V 9NQ
and Eljay Yildirim of
Thunderbolt, London

Research by: Rachel Wright
Consultants: Margaret Mulvihill
and Tim Wood
Watercolour artwork: Peter Kent
and Stuart Trotter
Computer artwork: D Oliver

© Two-Can Publishing Ltd, 1997

This edition published 1997 by:
Two-Can Publishing
in association with
Franklin Watts
96 Leonard Street
London
EC2A 4RH

Hardback ISBN 1-85434-408-0
Dewey Decimal Classification 930

2 4 6 8 10 9 7 5 3 1

A catalogue record for this book is
available from the British Library.

Printed in the USA by
R. R. Donnelley & Sons Co.

Photographic credits: Britstock-IFA
(West Stock Montgomery) p19, p21;
Bruce Coleman (MPL Fogden) p5;
C M Dixon p28r; e.t.archive p28l; Steve
Gorton p24; Michael Holford p8, p13r,
p15, (British Museum) p4bl, p6, p7, p9,
p12-13c, (Bardo Museum, Tunis) p14;
Tony Stone Images p20l; Werner
Forman Archive (British Museum) FC,
(Egyptian Museum, Cairo) p4tr,
(Metropolitan Museum of Art, N.Y.)
p20r, (Museum of Anthropology,
Mexico) p25, (Statens Historiska
Museum, Stockholm) p26; Zefa p22.